LIBERTY WALKS NAKED

Liberty Walks Naked

By

Maram Al Masri

translated by Theo Dorgan

SOUTHWORDeditions

First published in hardback in 2017
by Southword Editions,
The Munster Literature Centre,
Frank O'Connor House,
84 Douglas Street,
Cork, Ireland.
This paperback edition May 2018

www.munsterlit.ie
info@munsterlit.ie

Copyright © 2017 Maram Al Masri
English translations & foreword © 2017 Theo Dorgan

The moral rights of the authors have been asserted

ISBN 978-1-905002-58-0

for the White Helmets & Antonin

Contents

Under the Drip of Images *9*
Translator's Note *11*
On a school wall *13*
A woman complains to the Sultan *14*
I am a man, not an animal *15*
Selmieh, selmieh *16*
Have you seen him? *17*
My son is handsome *18*
Yes, yes *19*
On her four paws *20*
She takes your face *21*
The arms sloping *22*
When you see them *23*
As drunken boats *24*
She *25*
Over the temples *26*
The wooden boxes, wooden boxes *27*
15th March 2013: 5000 infants killed *28*
I do not want *29*
The children of Syria *30*
A sordid hospital ward *31*
A man covered in dust *32*
In a little Suzuki van *33*
It seems to me *34*
We, the exiled ones *35*
Where is Hassan? *36*
The over made up presenter *37*
An everyday scene *38*
Tell me a story *39*
In a memorial photo *40*
Study well, my daughter *41*
The Children of freedom *42*
I admit that I am sad *44*

15th March 2013: 5000 women in Syrian prisons *45*
15th March 2013: 1,364,268 refugees *46*
Where are you from? *47*
Liberty walks naked *48*
Cover it, cover it! *49*
I was walking, I was exhausted *50*
Syria for me *51*
Death falls as a great weight *52*
In the building where I grew up *53*
Poems have not served *54*
I should like to create a world *55*
Your face is a round white loaf *56*
In the market of the world *57*
Letter of an Arab Mother to her Son *58*
Archives of An Uncertain Life *60*

Under the Drip of Images

How to go on living without speaking of you, victims of the war for liberty in Syria? How can poetry justify its existence and give witness to the nobility of life unless it involve itself in the struggles of humanity?

Since the 15th of March 2011, the day spring began to flower in the heart of the Syrian people, drained by the long privations imposed by the dictatorship, the image of this risen people haunts me day and night. Not only because many of those who are dear to me still live there, but also because such courage, such strength of will, touches me profoundly.

Day and night, I have lived those months in the permanent drip of images and news flowing in from over there, via the Internet, via social media resources such as Facebook, through various media, especially Arab media, in videos, on Youtube, through the testimony of friends.

My body has been here, my soul there. I have felt joy and I have felt sorrow also. And, too, a sense of guilt that I have not been there, although I have lived in France for a long time now.

Poetry, that reality fragile as the perfume of jasmine, what can it do in the face of tanks? Yet, one knows that, in every epoch, poets and poetry have been in danger from dictators, from the murder of Callisthenes by Alexander the Great up to our own day, because language has a redoubtable power that all dictators fear.

Many may think that poetry is the business of imagination only, and that to paint pictures of the real world is banal. I call to mind what Bertolt Brecht did during the war, in *Manual of the German War*, where each quatrain is a commentary on a topical photograph clipped from the press. Not to glorify war, but to show to his contemporaries, and to generations then unborn, that war is the most terrible of realities. What is strange, is that I began this book before ever I discovered that book of Brecht's...

To capture a moment in words, to throw light on some 'detail', to 'arrest an image', this is a way of extracting from the movement of video an image which is then frozen on paper; it is to fix an instant and put it in perspective. By means of words, the poem gives life to the image and helps us make sense of it — and of course, it is my interpretation, granted. From my point of view, this also is poetry.

Despite the quotidian character of the horror, this cannot be made banal, cannot be made seem 'normal'.

My people are not engaged in a civil war, but in a democratic revolution that will end in triumph. This revolution has shown not just the atrocities of which the human being is capable but also the beauty and the nobility of numberless acts.

This book is an act of homage to those victims who have lost their lives to bombardment, killing and torture. It is also an homage to those families for whom no joy, not even that of victory, can ever erase the bitterness of having lost those whom they loved.

Up to this day in March 2013, there are more than 60,000 dead. It is hard to list all the names, even though I would like to inscribe each and every name in these pages. They are the dead of my people — and I do not forget those soldiers of the regular army who are themselves trapped into this violence. Above all, not to forget a single person. Just as there are 'unknown soldiers', there are many 'unknown' men and women and children. Peasants, doctors, artists... the very body of Syria itself has been martyred.

— Maram al-Masri

Translator's note

Maram al-Masri is, in normal circumstances (whatever those are), a poet of considerable lyrical gifts. In this present collection she has stripped her voice back to a bareness that plots a precise and elegant course between the twin dangers of the naive and the rhetorical registers. Acknowledging a stylistic kinship with certain poems of Bertolt Brecht, she says plainly that this way of suiting her poems to their occasions is a conscious, deliberate choice: the situation in Syria is so desperate, so overwhelming, that poetry must bend to a different imperative if it is to lift beyond despair into the plainest possible voice of witness. I have tried to accommodate that register in English.

The contemporary sensibility of English, if I might put it like this, shies away from what can seem overblown, excessively naive or florid; hence terms like 'martyr', apparently resistant to irony in Arabic, are problematic for us, the more so because the jihadist employment of the term has almost isolated the word from its long history of plain meaning. Maram al-Masri, long time resident in Paris, cosmopolitan, an ironist herself at times, finds herself forced by press of circumstance towards language that can sometimes read uncomfortably when translated into contemporary English. She acknowledges the difficulty when she speaks of her need to make

> "...a world naive
> and sincere
> as this poem."

The reader will, I hope, make the necessary accommodations when reading these translations.

The most difficult problem I had to face was, how to translate the term 'Liberté'. In English, 'Liberty' has not the weight of history, of hope, of certainty and expectation that informs the French term, the French usage.

The republican value of liberty, in the Francophone world, carries the freight of the Revolution, its premises and its promises.

When Patrick Henry, in March 1775, at the Virginia Convention, cried "Give me liberty, or give me death", he did not mean 'give me freedom from England', he meant, I think, something more like 'Let me live in freedom, let me experience freedom as the absolute ground of my life'.

Liberty, in this sense, is not usually what is meant by the word in Anglophone discourse; it is scarcely a constituting moral or political term, is more usually yoked with permission — one seeks liberty to plead a case in the Law Courts, one is at liberty to pursue a course of action, one's person is at liberty (that is to say free to move about, not detained or constrained) but implict in these usages is the idea of an authority which gives permission, an authority that *grants* liberty — whether that authority be a person or a provision in law.

Nevertheless, I have translated 'liberté' almost everywhere in this collection with the term 'liberty', the notabe exception occurring in poem 30, "Les enfants de la liberté', where 'freedom' seems a more appropriate word. Mostly, though, the term 'freedom' is inadequate to carry the often-desperate charge that 'liberté', sometimes 'Liberté', has for al-Masri.

— Theo Dorgan
   Dublin 2016

On a school wall...

On a school wall
the word liberty written in white chalk
by the small hands of children.

On the wall of History
liberty has written their names
in blood.

A woman complains to the Sultan...

A woman complains to the Sultan
that his soldiers have stolen her cattle
while she was sleeping.
The Sultan says to her:
you should be guarding your herd,
not sleeping.
She replies:
I thought, Highness, that you were watching over us...
and so I slept.

I am a man, not an animal...

I am a man, not an animal,
cries the ordinary citizen
Ahmad Abdouwhab

in his trembling voice —
a prisoner escaped
from the cage of fear.
The veins in his throat
are swollen
and his eyes drown in rage.

He has never read
Balzac or Victor Hugo,
knows nothing of Marx or Lenin...

On this day
the ordinary citizen
Ahmad Abdouwhab
becomes extraordinary.

Selmieh, selmieh...

Selmieh, selmieh
Peaceful, peaceful
They come out singing of peace
bare-chested, with clean hands.

Houriah, houriah
Liberty, liberty
They appear crying liberty
bare-chested, with roses in their hands.

Yes this is a chant to shiver
the solid heart of fear,
to make the mask of the raven fall.

Have you seen him?...

Have you seen him?

Carrying his infant in his arms
advancing with magisterial step
head up, back straight...

As if the infant should be happy and proud
to be carried like this in his father's arms...

If only he was
alive.

My son is handsome...

"My son is handsome.
My son is a hero.
The dictatorship
is jealous of heroes.

He is a hero and my love,
the light of my eyes."

She turns with him, proud,
and shows him to those others who weep.

In her arms, her son
smiling in the frame
of the photo.

Yes, yes...

Yes, yes,
embrace him again
and again.
Yes, yes,
touch him again and again.
Yes, yes,
take him again in your arms
as if for the last time.

But it is the last time
that your lips
will touch him,
the last time the scent of him will fill you,
the last time that your tears will wash
his warm body.

On her four paws...

On her four paws
she advances
like a wounded tigress.

She crawls on the ground
to catch hold of your foot
as they draw you towards your burial.

Why does she stop them
stealing you
from the tomb?

She takes your face...

She takes your face
between her hands,
then she kisses you,
crushing her mouth.

You shall be buried,
O my martyr,
with your mother's lips
fixed to your skin.

The arms sloping...

The arms sloping,
hands opening gently to the sky,
like someone who has not found,
even in the house of God,
an answer to his questions.

I think that he has turned
a thousand times on himself
because despair
has struck him.
Despair
has killed him,
just as the bombs have killed his children.

When you see them...

When you see them,
do not lower your head.
Look at them
even behind your clouded eyes.

Perhaps then in their cruel death
they will repose in the paradise
of your memory.

As drunken boats...

As drunken boats
on the ocean
balance themselves
from right to left,
from left to right,
heads roll in a circle
from high to low,
from low to high.
Cries and moans.
Why and how?

Do you hear
their sad song
as you are stretched out
with your arms
crossed on your breast?

She...

She:
Mother, what is liberty?

Her mother:
Something very dear.

She:
So, can we buy it, us?

Her mother:
That is why they make us pay for it with our lives.

Over the temples...

Over the temples
points of light multiply,
veins pulse and beat.
Cold metal
is poised there.

The warmth of the body does not stop him
pressing down on the safety catch,
blind with hate.

The killer films the scene
with pride.

The wooden boxes, wooden boxes...

The wooden boxes, wooden boxes
lifting themselves lightly
as if they were made of air.
They turn, turn...
they dance with themselves,
they sing
songs that break out in the sky,
melting the mountains of sorrow.

They turn, turn
as if they had wings,
they fly as if dancing
from shoulder to shoulder,
they climb, they climb,
they fall...

Boxes of bare wood
austere as the death of the poor.
Inside, muffled cries,
closed-eye dreams,
smiles that will not see lips.
Inside, wet faces,
the kisses of an orphan mother.
Coffins, coffins,
costly gifts
for the wedding of liberty.

15th March 2013: 5000 infants killed...

It is not from his mother's womb
that this new-born emerges,
it is from the womb of earth.

This is not a prehistoric figurine,
this is a baby buried
by a bomb.

He did not have even time
to take his first
feed.

I do not want...

I do not want
these chemicals,
I am allergic

said a four year old girl,
scratching her skin.

The children of Syria...

The children of Syria
swaddled in their shrouds
like wrapped sweets.
But, they are not made of sugar,
they are made of flesh
and dreams
and love.

The streets await you,
gardens, schools and holidays
await you,
children of Syria.

It is too soon to be birds,
to play
in the heavens.

A sordid hospital ward...

A sordid hospital ward:
a wounded person laid out on a soiled bed.
A man with a notebook and pen
approaches the wounded one
and demands: it was the outlaw army
shot you?
No, says the wounded one.
The man perseveres:
Sign here to say it was the outlaw army
who shot you.
No, says the wounded one.
A gun is put to his head:
Sign here!
No, it was the regular army.

A shot explodes.

A man covered in dust...

A man covered in dust
sits on a pavement,
looking away.
On his knees
a baby, its pallor luminous,
shakes his arms, his hands,
as it drinks
from the baby bottle the man holds to its mouth.

Behind them
a young boy
clutches a bag of bread
tight to his chest
— he, too, is gazing away.

In another corner of the scene,
two silhouettes:
A child seated against the door
of a destroyed house,
a woman kneeling before him,
trying to calm his terror.

This is not a scene from a movie:
this is a family
in Syria today.

In a little Suzuki van...

In a little Suzuki van
he has laid out his dead wife,
settling her clothing
as if she were asleep.

Placed on the seat, above,
the bag of bread
she had set out to find
so that today their children might eat,
so that her death
might serve some purpose.

It seems to me...

It seems to me
there is mourning somewhere.
I am wearing black
even though
this is not my place.

It seems to me
there is celebration somewhere.
I am happy
even though
this is not my place.

We, the exiled ones...

We, the exiled ones,
who live on anti-depressants,
Facebook has become our homeland,
it opens the sky
they close in our faces
at the frontiers.

We, the exiled ones,
we sleep clutching to ourselves
our mobile phones.
In the light
of our computer screens
we doze off full of sorrow,
we wake full of hope.

We, the exiled ones,
we circle our distant houses
as lovers circle prisons,
hoping to see the shadows
of their loved ones.

We, the exiled, we are sick
with an incurable sickness.

To love a homeland
is a death sentence.

Where is Hassan?...

- Where is Hassan?
- He is there, your brother, we will heal Hassouneh.

(The camera moves towards little Hassan, laid out on a table: a bomb has mangled his arms.)

- And me?
- We will heal you, too.
- But, I'm afraid of the needle.
- We won't prick you if you promise not to be afraid.
- Give me some medicine that tastes like lemon jam.
- We'll give you the medicine that tastes like lemon jam.

(The camera shows the little girl's two arms, mangled by a bomb.)

- Ask my Daddy to ask my mother to bring me a dress.
- We will give you a dress.
- But, you have a shop here?
- Yes, and we have something even more important.
- Yes? What else?
- Lots of bread.
- And what else?
- Dresses.
- And what else?

(The little girl is wide-eyed. We hear the doctor, answering.)

- We have God.

The over made up presenter...

The over made up presenter
demands of the crouching child:
— Who is that woman
stretched in her blood
beside you?
The child answers:
my mother.

The television presenter looks into the camera
and smiles,
— Who is that man stretched in his blood
beside you:
The child answers:
my father.

The State television presenter, preening:
-—And this baby?
My sister.
Her name is Houriah*.

She was born yesterday.

* Houriah = Liberty

An everyday scene...

An everyday scene:
A queue outside a bakery,
sound of explosions.

Everyone runs,
even the trees snatch at their roots, trying to run.

But not hunger.
Hunger doesn't care any more,
continues to wait
to buy
bread.

Tell me a story...

Tell me a story,
demands the child
born in a prison
to a raped mother.

The visitor begins:
Once upon a time there was
a young boy who lived
in a house
with windows
looking out on a calm street.

What is *window?*
the child interrupts.

It is a hole in the wall
where the sun comes in
and where birds
perch.

What is *bird?*
the child aks.

The visitor picks up a pencil
and draws on the wall
a window,
and a child
with wings.

In a memorial photo...

In a memorial photo
a twenty year old youngster
lies stretched in the middle of a field;
among the green plants of his village
he poses, proud of his youth.

He does not know,
or perhaps he does know,
that soon he will feed
their sap.

STUDY WELL, MY DAUGHTER...

Study well, my daughter
your country needs what you will build.

Would you like a coffee?
Some tea?

You will succeed, I'm sure of it,
you will have your degree.
How happy I shall be —
I will make you a great celebration,
Ah yes...engineer... such a fine profession...

She left for the university
loaded with pens and dreams.

One of her shoes came home
in her mother's hands.

THE CHILDREN OF FREEDOM...

The children of freedom
do not dress themselves in *Petit Bateau*.
Their skin quickly gets used to rough fabric.
The children of freedom
have second-hand clothes
and shoes too big for their feet.
Often they dress in naked air or earth.

The children of freedom
do not know the taste of a banana
or a strawberry.
They eat dry bread
soaked in the water of patience.

When evening comes,
the children of freedom
do not take baths,
they do not blow soap bubbles.
They play with tyres, with pebbles,
the debris of bombs.

Before they go to sleep
the children of freedom
do not brush their teeth,
they do not listen to fairy tales
of prince and princess.

They hear the noises of fear, of cold,
on the pavements outside their destroyed houses,
in the camps of neighbouring countries
or
in the tombs.

The children of freedom
wait, like
all other children in the world,
for their mother to come home.

I ADMIT THAT I AM SAD...

I admit that I am sad.
For days now I have not opened
the window of my soul.

I admit that I am sad,
like the mother of a prisoner,
like the widow of a martyr,
the mother of an orphan.

I admit that I am sad in a time
when sorrow is not permitted us,
where we are coerced into a PR campaign
for joy and strength.

I admit that I am sad
and I love this sorrow
that is dedicated to you.

I admit that I am sad,
I wish for no consolation except
an end to these killings.

15th March 2013: 5,000 women in Syrian prisons

What do you do, my sisters,
when your breasts swell
and harden with pain?

When suffering
tears
your belly?

When sorrow overfloods you

so that the blood
flowing between your legs
blackens and crusts?

What do you do about the smell?

How do you manage, my sisters,
when your periods come
in the prisons so cold
and so dark?

The prisons where you are beaten and tortured,
the prisons where you are
crowded together,
chained together?

What do you do, my sisters,
when rage rises behind your eyes?

15th March 2013: 1,364,268 refugees

What do they carry with them, the refugees?

They gather up in a hurry
what they can of their possessions,
they stuff them
into plastic bags
torn as their lives,
old as their fears.

Or perhaps they bundle them into a sheet...
Perhaps they will not have had time
even to string their shoes together...

The refugees flee death
but they hear its echoing steps always behind them.
They flee with their bags
and the hope of returning.

They will cross the borders
only to find that all they have carried with them
has fallen away
through a hole in the bag.

Where are you from?...

— Where are you from?
— Syria.
— From which city in Syria?
— I was born in Dara. I grew up in Homs. I blossomed in Lattakia, grew young again in Banias. I flowered in Jesr Alsoghor. I burned in Hama. I was blown up in Edleb, I was bombed in Aleppo. I was thunder in Déralzur, lightning over Qamishli.

Massacred at Daraya.

— Who are you?
— I am the one who frightens them
  I am the one whom they imprison
  I am the one they set on fire
  I am the one who is killed.

It is I...
who causes the heart's tree to flower
as I pass,
I who bring down the mountain from its hauteur,
I who make history retrace its steps,
I who colour the earth with my sun.

It is I...
she who speaks out in the face of the dictator
she who lives only in noble spirits
she who is not to be bought, is not for sale.

I am the bread of life, and life's milk.

My name is
Liberty.

Liberty walks naked…

Liberty walks naked
out of the mountains of Syria,
into the refugee camps.
Her feet sink in the mud
and her hands are chapped from the cold,
from the pain.
But, she advances.

She goes by,
her children linked in her arms.
They fall in the path —
she weeps,
yet she goes forward.

Break her feet,
she advances,
always she advances.
Slash her throat,
you will not stop her song.

Cover it, cover it!...

Cover it, cover it!

My heart quakes
like a newborn child,
abandoned,
torn
from the womb of her nation,
naked.

I was walking, I was exhausted.

I was walking, I was exhausted.
I looked behind me
and saw I was dragging
a mountain of sorrow with my right hand,
a mountain of hope with my left.

Syria for me...

Syria for me
is a bleeding wound.
It is my mother on her death-bed
it is my slaughtered childhood
it is my nightmare and my hope
it is my sleeplessness and my waking.

Syria for me
is an abandoned orphan,
a woman violated night after night
by an an ancient monster,
raped, locked up,
forced into marriage.

Syria for me
is suffering humanity,
is a beautiful woman singing an ode to liberty —
but her throat has been cut.

It is the people of the rainbow
who will shine out
after the storm, after the lightning.

Death falls as a great weight...

Death falls as a great weight
on those hiding under the bed.
They hear it whistling down, they ask
who will it fall on this time?

Death comes of a sudden
but sometimes as slow as a steamroller,
delighting to hear the cries,
the wailing.

The death-storm
comes to sweep them away,
the crowd in the queue
to buy fuel oil.

The death-plume comes
and sends flying
souls heavy with suffering,
to free them from weight of sorrow,
from so long a torture.

Death comes in a robe of frozen snow,
to cover the bloody face
of earth.

In the building where I grew up

In the building where I grew up
Mother Ali
opens the cage of the sun
with her smile,
Mother Muhammad
shakes from the carpet
troubles and worries,
Mother Georges
adorns with white lace
her daughter's dresses
for going to church.
Nearby, Mother Azad
is ironing shawl and shabek,
Father Zven in his shop
is sewing a fine suit
for the party
of his neighbour Mustapha.

In my country,
coloured
with mountains and valleys,
with plains and forests,
there is the sea, there are rivers
there are mosques and churches,
synagogues and bars,
there are Sunni and Alaouite,
Druze and Ismaelites,
Shiites and non-believers.
All colours, all nuances,
gathered into a single homeland.

Poems have not served...

Poems have not served
Songs have not served
Dance has not served
Tears and crying have not served
Children's smiles have not served —
They have not served, Daraya,
your roses and olive branches
for the soldiers of death.
Not your magnificent candles,
Great Lady of Salamieh,
nor your bread, Halfaya,
nothing has served
to hold back the oncoming tanks.

I should like to create a world...

I should like to create a world
where there are no longer weapons
or war,
a world where a mother
will love the child of another
as her own son,
a world that will not distinguish
between men,
a new world
where neither glory
nor losses will matter.

I would like to create a world
where no human being will go unhoused,
where none shall die
of cold or of hunger.

I would like to create a world
where I becomes we,
and we shall be I,
a world naive
and sincere
as this poem.

Your face is a round white loaf...

Your face is a round white loaf
into which the blood of liberty has sunk.
Your famished body mixes into the earth
becoming an icon for this century.
Your blood has drawn the frontiers that separate
justice from injustice.
It is the pure blood that flows
with the birth of liberty.

In the market of the world...

In the market of the world,
I see you, my country,
chained and naked
on the stalls —
and all around swarm
the prospective buyers with their offers;
they promise you a good marriage,
new chains
fashioned from gold.

The merchants and vultures
are gathered to eat your flesh.
Up for auction: your children, your women,
your young, your future,
your prestige, your history.

O Syria,
we will wash away your blood
in the milk of our love.

Letter of an Arab Mother to her Son

Liberty
is a cord snapping
in a chest
that can take no more.
It is the song of sirens
to brave sailors.

Liberty
is the Beauty of beauties,
mistress of strength,
goddess of wisdom.
You must give her your love.

She is the paradise of fire
that starts from a spark
as the poem from a word,
as love from a kiss.
She is the richness of richness.
You must become her.

My son, be the drop of water
that joins with other drops
to make a wave
washing the shores of the world,
smoothing the jagged rocks.

My son, be the breath that diffuses into air
so that the storm may rip up
the roots of injustice.
Be the spark
of light,
that the sun may illumine your country.

Your life is dear to me,
like the lives of all children to their mothers.
My son, I dedicate you
to Liberty.

Archives of An Uncertain Life

— Yes, I lived in despite of death I was born, I grew, and like all Syrians I loved, I married, I had children in spite of death. I have never wished to live elsewhere: for a long time I had the conviction that to live in Syria would be an act of heroism. So, today what do you think it is?

— We have lived in death. Now, while we are in the process of emerging from its belly, its umbilical cord wraps around our neck.

— I live in death.
I have done nothing else but live as a witness, I have decided I will not bear false witness.

— The human being is not perfect, I tell myself this watching a flight of birds seek the horizon.
No matter what bird I might be,
I am tired of being glued to the earth.

— All that for which I have lived and all I have made is here.
I do not think I could die in some other place.
There is no meaning to living somewhere
if there is no meaning to dying in that place.

They said to me: "Stop all that and look to where the sun is."
I looked, and I saw the sun on the horizon
in the process of eclipse.

— Monzer Masri*

*Translator's note:
Brother to Maram al-Masri, Monzer Masri lives in Lattakia.

www.ingramcontent.com/pod-product-compliance
Lightning Source LLC
Chambersburg PA
CBHW051717040426
42446CB00008B/923